A Passage Through The Land Of Sleepy Hollow

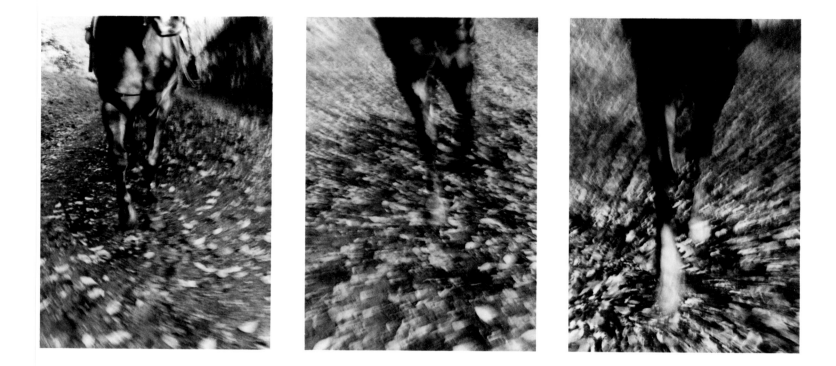

To Dr. George Hyman my loving father, humanitarian, and supporter of my work, and

to William H. whose courage, grace and love of life are the heart of the matter.-L.H.B., M.G.F. and A.C.G.

A Passage Through The Land Of Sleepy Hollow

Story and Photographs by Lynn Hyman Butler
Edited by Mimi Forer

Glover Press 1988

I would like to thank the following people who have worked with and encouraged me in the making of this book; Robert Blake as a special teacher, Charles Stainback, Bert Miller, Philip Pocock, Daniel Kazimierski, David Spear and Eugene Richards.-L.H.B.

Orders for this book should be addressed to Glover Press.
Copyright © Glover Press, 1988
500 County Avenue, Secaucus, NJ 07094

Book design by Mimi Forer
Printed by Morgan Press, Inc.

Library of Congress Cataloging in Publication Data

Butler, Lynn Hyman, 1953-
  A passage through the land of Sleepy Hollow

  Summary: Photographs accompany this retelling of Irving's classic tale of a headless horseman.
  1. Horses--Fiction. [1. Ghost--Fiction.
2. New York (State)--Fiction] I. Forer, Mimi, 1953-   . II. Irving, Washington, 1783-1859. Legend of Sleepy Hollow. III. Title.
PS3552. U8263P37 1988   [Fic]   87-37945
ISBN 0-944782-00-0

Manufactured in the USA

Introduction

There are places where dreams still flourish. Where legends are believed as truth. Such a place is Tarrytown. A historic and peaceful village on the Eastern shore of the Hudson River in the state of New York.

Tarrytown began as a Dutch settlement, named by the wives of those farmers who tarried in the local taverns on market day. It is one of those magical parts of the world where the atmosphere is steeped with the intermingling of history and fantasy. Here, as in days long ago, fact is fancy and all creatures, man and beast, believe in tales of evil spirits, ghosts and goblins. It was here that Washington Irving wrote *The Legend of Sleepy Hollow*, a story set in this dreamy land whose citizens glory in the far fetched.

As the legend goes, a headless horseman rides throughout the land in search of his head, lost to a cannonball in the Revolutionary War. A gentleman named Ichabod Crane was said to have met this horseman on a dark and windy October night. Ichabod, the village schoolmaster and local expert on witchcraft, was also the rather superstitious choirmaster of the Old Dutch Church. (He was often heard singing psalms loudly to himself to calm the fright he always felt at night when he returned home from an evening of socializing with some local family). He was a popular guest for his vivid storytelling in the cozy farm houses along the Hudson.

Ichabod spent many winter evenings by the fire with some of the "Old Dutch wives," sharing tales and ghoststories of haunted places and especially of the headless horseman.

Ichabod fell in love with a beautiful and wealthy young woman, Katrina Van Tassel. The daughter of a local and prosperous farmer, a marriage to her would seem to provide a life of unbelievable luxury. In fact, her wealth and the dreams of splendour it conjured up were equally if not more appealing to him than the woman herself. As she must have known, he did not love her, and she fell in love with another. Ichabod met his fate on the night that Katrina rejected him. He departed from her home, quietly furious into the dark night; his imagination brimming full of the tales of ghosts and mysterious happenings. It was on this ride that he was pursued by a Hessian trooper, who carried his head and finally threw it full force at Ichabod, knocking him to the ground...

Though Irving made it clear that Ichabod's encounter was in fact with his jealous and mischievious rival, what happens afterwards, the legend provides...And though the evidence of the pumpkin, (mistaken for the head of the horseman) and the saddle of the old schoolmaster, Ichabod, were found on the ground the following day, the fair folk of the Hudson Valley are entranced by magic and fantastic adventure. While Ichabod may not have actually encountered the ghost rider, many believe that to this day the horseman still roams the land.

All who dwell there breathe this magical atmosphere and have their own stories to tell, their truths to share about this historic and beautiful place. Here follows then, one horse's tale of the Legend of Sleepy Hollow....

This may be a dream.

There lives a horse, Knickerbocker, strong and sleek.
He rides through a valley
called Sleepy Hollow.

Full of wonder and joy at the world's beauty is he.

A fine animal who harbors no fear, no superstition.
Only bliss and curiosity guide his journey
through the wild life of this enchanted land.

Knickerbocker told me this story, an old one.
"You will learn from this...
There are many ways to enter into this life.
You will find that you have the choice."

We rode on, horse and rider.
A strange tale is unfolding,
but then, we are in a magical place.

This is the tale.
A man went through life always afraid,
expecting the worst.
His name was Ichabod Crane.
A perfect name for a lanky schoolmaster.
Tall and thin, all arms and legs
and crookedness of features.

You can easily imagine him, all those years ago.
There had been the legend,
a story of a headless rider
roaming the countryside.
Here, where we are now.

The horseman was often seen rushing past an old church....

to get back to the churchyard
before daybreak, after a night of searching.

"But let me tell you more of my story," Knick continued.
"The shadow of the headless horseman appears and fades,
speckled like the sun through leaves."

"Tricking the eye and fooling the senses.
Flicker and vanish.
I see the shadow of the fabled horse and rider of long ago."

.....There is no threat, no fear.
The shadow is only silent and fast.
Here, and then gone.

Why should we be afraid of this horse
and his strange passenger?

There are soft earthen trails
through greens so lightened and
a river so vast it was mistaken for a wider sea.
A resting place.
A green respite from the noisy confusion
of the city further south.

Charm and sparkle.
Glitter fine green,
so woody and vast.

Countryside so peaceful,
all fable and fancy
grow as wild and free as the pasture rose.

Deer startle and vanish
Like the shadow, quick.

Curly sheep look up briefly,
then go back to grazing,
content.

All the creatures rouse from a slumber quiet
to something different as
the shadow passes by.

Amid today's tangle of highways and huge bridgespans,
these lush hills are still full
of promise and excitement,
of life unseen by humankind.

One can still find a wilderness here.

Things still go on unexplained.

Knick brought me back from my daydreaming.
"Look at it this way," he said.....

"You can fly through life.
Make it all your Sleepy Hollow.
Even if it isn't entirely a place of good dreams.
The secret is in your eye.
The secret is the way one looks at things."

"Knick, Knick, Knick," I said.
"This is foolish fancy."
Could a horse know so much?
As if hearing these doubts, he replied,

"I think you'd like to find out
how I was chosen to know all this.
Ah, but that's my secret. A horse has legends as well.
Have faith in me.
They say there is truth in every fiction".....

The sun was falling, low and warm.
Indian Summer, this fine October afternoon.

"See your shadow? He looked like that,"
Knick went on. "No head. Riding.
They say he was angry, searching."

We stopped at the river for a drink.
I saw my shadow.
It made me shiver. Silly.
As he drank, I thought about Ichabod, this man
that Knick seemed to know so much about and

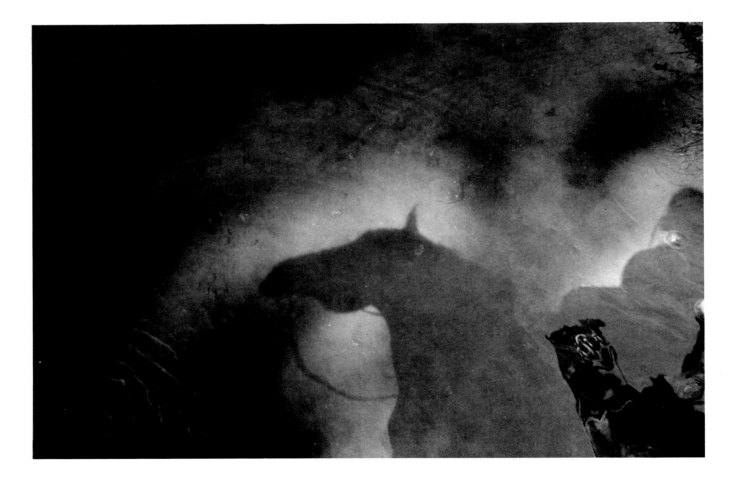

the shadow that frightened him
into disappearing forever.
Knick knew that
the real illusion was fear,
and in the darkness,
fears, like shadows, are real.

We paused to let a carriage pass.
"It was a time then, remember, of horses.
It was our day…"
Knick sighed dreamily.
And for a minute he seemed distant, almost leaving me.

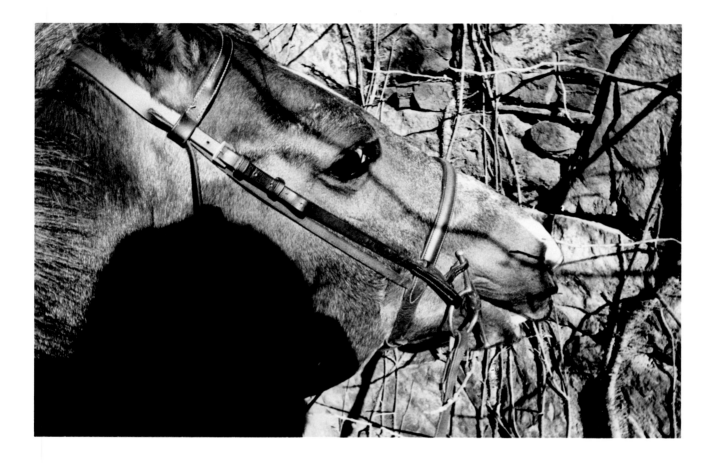

In remembering that beautiful time, he was nearly sad.
But then Knick was never sad. Never.
"Except for my magic, I am simple," he said.

His eyes smiled.
"I need to be cared for now. Warm shelter.
Good food. The love of another,
that too."

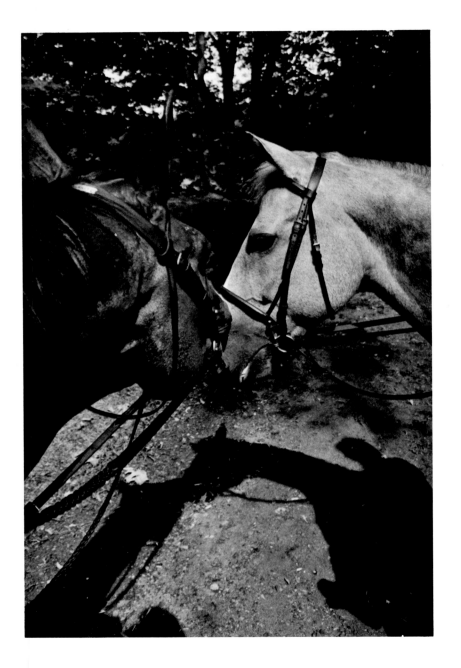

Civilized man can make things so complicated.

Now Knick was cooled from his drink
and we rode on.
The trail became more lovely. More lonely.

He spoke to me
again.
"These golden woods
gleaming on the Hudson's shore
have been home to all sorts
of strange events and magic."

"The woods still stand, shelter for us all.
Who will protect their history?
We too stand to lose something we may have never truly possessed."

"I am no longer wild," he said,
"as you are not."

"What about the wildness of this land?"
The shadow passed again, I thought.

I was startled.

Like a cloud passing before the sun,
the shadow enveloped us and we were one.
Knick's eyes were bright.

As he rose up fiercely, his words echoed.
"The only shadow one need fear is that of an empty life,
of dreams spoiled by greed, unfulfilled,
and turned to nightmares of things not done.
It is not by magic alone that beauty prevails."

Don't look back, there is no time.

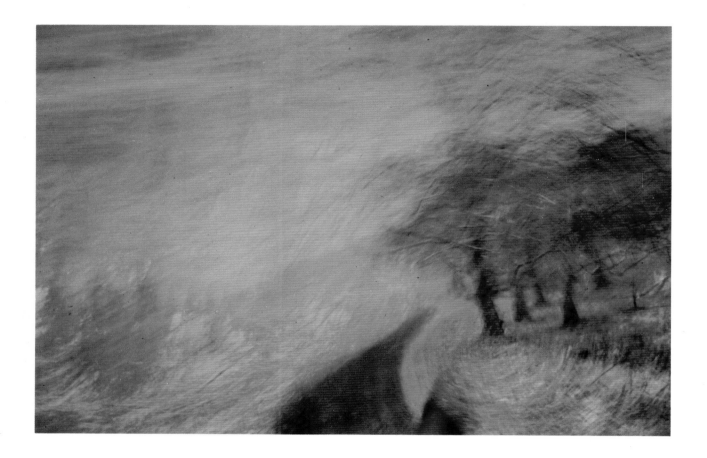

And Knick was gone.